CAN YOU UNCOVER THE OAK ISLAND MONEY PIT?

AN INTERACTIVE TREASURE ADVENTURE

BY MATTHEW K. MANNING

CAPSTONE PRESS
a capstone imprint

Published by Capstone Press, an imprint of Capstone
1710 Roe Crest Drive
North Mankato, Minnesota 56003
capstonepub.com

Copyright © 2024 by Capstone. All rights reserved. No part of this publication may
be reproduced in whole or in part, or stored in a retrieval system, or transmitted
in any form or by any means, electronic, mechanical, photocopying, recording, or
otherwise, without written permission of the publisher.

Library of Congress Cataloging-in-Publication Data
Names: Manning, Matthew K., author.
Title: Can you uncover the Oak Island money pit? : an interactive treasure
    adventure / by Matthew K. Manning.
Description: North Mankato, MN : Capstone Press, [2024] | Series: You choose:
    treasure hunters | Includes bibliographical references. | Audience: Ages 8 to 12.
    Audience: Grades 4-6.
Summary: You are intrigued by the legend of Oak Island, Nova Scotia, and
    determined to search out its secrets, and the reader will decide which of the many
    choices and clues you will follow—to become the discoverer of the truth or the
    seventh victim of the curse of Oak Island.
Identifiers: LCCN 2022050312 (print) | LCCN 2022050313 (ebook) |
    ISBN 9781669031956 (hardcover) | ISBN 9781669031925 (paperback)
    ISBN 9781669031932 (pdf)
Subjects: LCSH: Oak Island Treasure Site (N.S.)—Juvenile literature. | Treasure
    troves—Nova Scotia—Oak Island (Lunenburg)—Juvenile literature. | Oak Island
    (Lunenburg, N.S.)—History—Juvenile literature. | Plot-your-own stories.
    LCGFT: Choose-your-own stories.
Classification: LCC F1039.O35 M36 2024 (print) | LCC F1039.O35 (ebook)
    DDC 971.6/23—dc23/eng/20230216
LC record available at https://lccn.loc.gov/2022050312
LC ebook record available at https://lccn.loc.gov/2022050313

Editorial Credits
Editor: Aaron Sautter; Designer: Bobbie Nuytten; Media Researcher:
Rebekah Hubstenberger; Production Specialist: Whitney Schaefer

Photo Credits
Alamy: gary corbett, 46, Tango Images, 102; Getty Images: Bill Tompkins, 104,
DigitalGlobe/ScapeWare3d, 6, 106–107, Hulton Archive, 92, iStock/clu, 18,
iStock/Dony, 23, iStock/Mark Howard, 44, skynesher, 61, Stephen Frink, 81; Jo
Atherton, 8, 49, 76; Shutterstock: A_Dozmorov, cover , 1, Adwo, 12, 72, Andrey_
Kuzmin, design element (map), Celli07, 38, Ivan Kurmyshov, 87, Klintsou Ihar, 63,
Milkovasa, 28, Net Vector, design element (light), Patrick Thomas, cover (light),
Raimo Bergroth, 33, Salienko Evgenii, 67, SONGPAN JANTHONG, 28 (skull),
ZAX_77, 57; The Metropolitan Museum of Art: The Cloisters Collection, 1950, 41

All internet sites appearing in back matter were available and accurate when this
book was sent to press.

Printed and bound in the USA. PO#5425

TABLE OF CONTENTS

ABOUT YOUR ADVENTURE

YOU are a modern-day treasure hunter. You've learned about Oak Island near the coast of Nova Scotia, Canada. The mysterious island is rumored to hide many legendary treasures.

Your job is to decide where and how to search for Oak Island's buried secrets. Will you find lost treasures, or will you fall victim to the island's supposed curse? Your choices will decide if you strike it rich—or strike out.

Chapter One sets the scene. Then you choose which path to read. Follow the directions at the bottom of the page as you read the stories. The decisions you make determine what happens next. After you finish one path, go back and read the others for new perspectives and more adventures. Good luck on the hunt!

Turn the page to begin your adventure.

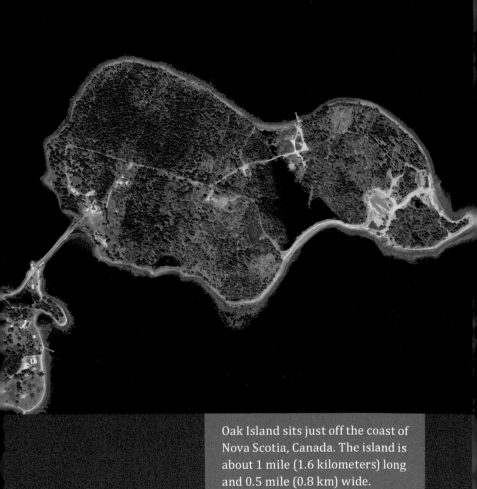

Oak Island sits just off the coast of Nova Scotia, Canada. The island is about 1 mile (1.6 kilometers) long and 0.5 mile (0.8 km) wide.

Chapter 1

CENTURIES OF SEARCHING

When you were young, you found an old magazine that described a mysterious place called Oak Island. This small island is home to the longest-running treasure hunt in history.

Oak Island is located in Mahone Bay. Pirates were known to frequent the area in the 1700s. Famed pirate Captain Kidd was thought to have hidden his fortune on one of the bay's many islands. Rumors about buried treasure soon spread among nearby towns.

In 1795, a young man named Daniel McGinnis was exploring Oak Island when he stumbled upon the top layer of a man-made pit. McGinnis and two friends soon began to dig into this pit.

Turn the page.

Some reports say that at 10 feet (3 meters) down, a platform of oak logs was found. Ten feet below that was another identical platform. This continued every ten feet until they reached the 90-foot (27-meter) mark.

At that point, a flat stone inscribed with strange markings was discovered. The story goes on to say that when this stone was removed, the shaft flooded with water. This stopped the treasure hunt in its tracks. The pit was too flooded to dig any deeper.

Since then, the pit's exact location seems to have been lost over the years. The area has been dug up so much that any signs of the original pit have long since vanished. But many still believe that treasure hides deep in this hole that many now call the Money Pit.

Other areas of Oak Island have attracted treasure hunters over the years as well. Smith's Cove is said to be a man-made beach. Box-like channels were supposedly built under the beach. It's thought that they supplied ocean water to act as a booby trap in the Money Pit.

A swamp on the island is also rumored to be artificial. Perhaps it was flooded to hide an underground treasure chamber.

Turn the page.

A large swampy area sits in the middle of Oak Island.

One other feature on the island was definitely made by people. On property belonging to treasure hunter Fred Nolan, several boulders were placed in the shape of a giant cross. The large stone at the center resembles the shape of a man's skull.

Many spots on Oak Island seem ripe for treasure hunting. It's your job to decide how best to explore the island's many secrets.

You could rent a home from a local resident and explore the island on your own. Or you can join an excavation crew and secretly look for a chance to uncover the treasure. Or perhaps you could scuba dive off the island's coast and look for an entrance to an underground cavern.

However, legends state that seven people will die searching for the island's riches. Six explorers have already lost their lives to the island.

Will you find the lost treasure, or will you become the seventh and final victim of Oak Island?

To rent a home on Oak Island, turn to page 13.

To join an excavation crew, turn to page 47.

To explore the waters off Oak Island's coast, turn to page 73.

A single road, called a causeway,
connects Oak Island to the mainland.

CHAPTER 2

THE HOUSE IN THE WOODS

You smile when you see the causeway stretch out in front of you. Once you cross this man-made road connecting the mainland to Oak Island, you'll finally be at your destination. It's been a long drive from your headquarters in New York City. But if you can unlock even one of the island's many mysteries, you'll leave as a very happy treasure hunter.

In a few short minutes, you pull up to what will be your home for the next few months. It's a modest two-story white house. According to the website where you booked your stay, this home is one of the oldest structures on Oak Island.

Turn the page.

You pull your car onto the gravel driveway next to the house. Salty air fills your lungs as you open the car door and stretch. Behind the house are dark, shadowy woods. Even in the bright afternoon sunshine, it looks a little eerie. You wonder what it'll look like tonight from your rented bedroom window.

"Well, hello there," says a voice with a thick Canadian accent. "You must be my new renter."

You turn to see a middle-aged man in a turtleneck and jeans. "I'm Evan," he says. "I've got your key for you."

"Thanks," you say, taking the key. You put it in your pocket, hoping you don't lose it.

"Before I go, I just want to be sure of one thing," says Evan. His face turns from friendly to very serious. "You said in your email that you were just here for a vacation, correct?"

"Oh, uh . . ." you stammer. "That's right."

"Because I've had enough of these would-be treasure hunters tearing up the place," Evan says.

You nod. You're not about to blow your cover. But you are indeed a treasure hunter by trade. You came to Oak Island to explore its secrets. There must be some truth to the legends of pirate gold here.

Or perhaps the island hides something even more exciting. Maybe you'll find clues to the Holy Grail, the legendary cup that Jesus Christ used at the Last Supper. Or perhaps you'll find the lost manuscripts of William Shakespeare, or even French queen Marie Antoinette's missing jewels. All of these treasures have been rumored to be buried somewhere on this mysterious island.

"Any damage to the house or property will be added to your bill in full," says Evan.

Turn the page.

You nod again and do your best to produce a fake smile.

"Well then, I'll leave you to it!" Evan says through a giant grin.

He waves and walks by you toward the street. There's not another car parked anywhere in sight. You wonder where Evan is headed. But soon enough, he disappears over a nearby hill.

"Huh, that's weird," you say quietly to yourself. Then you turn to look back at the property.

To explore the old house, go to page 17.
To head into the woods, turn to page 19.

The house's front door is unlocked, so you don't even need your key. You step inside and are surprised at how modern it looks. Evan must have done a lot of work on this place to keep it up to date for his renters. Vacationing on Oak Island must be more popular than you had thought.

On the first floor, there's a small kitchen, living room, and bathroom. You head upstairs and find a large bedroom. Above the bed, you see a trap door. You think it probably pulls down to allow access to an attic.

You walk back downstairs and see two doors in the corner of the room. Opening one door, you find a small closet. Then you try the other door's knob. It's locked. So you try the house key in your pocket.

Turn the page.

Old houses often have mysterious winding staircases.

It fits. You turn the key and hear a click. You open the door to see a dark staircase that must lead down to the basement.

The house is small. But it already seems to have its share of secrets. If you explore further, maybe you'll find some interesting clues.

To explore the basement, turn to page 21.
To head up to the attic, turn to page 25.

You don't even bother to take your suitcase out of the car. You're too excited to explore Oak Island.

You doubt that even the oldest home would hold any clues to buried treasure. If anything is hidden on this mysterious island, you think it will likely be somewhere in the woods. So you make your way to the trees to begin your hike.

There's not too much to see at first. The small forest is beautiful, but not unlike any other patch of Canadian wilderness. However, there's something unsettling about these woods. You keep pausing every few yards. You swear you hear footsteps behind you.

Every time you turn around, there's no one there. Your imagination must be getting the better of you.

Turn the page.

You follow a narrow deer trail to avoid most of the overgrowth. Before long, the dirt path splits into two directions.

You decide to pause and study your surroundings. The faint trickling of water can be heard to your left. To your right, the path seems to get darker.

Then you hear a rustling sound behind you in the bushes. It's best to keep moving, but which path should you take?

To go toward the sound of water, turn to page 27.

To take the darker path, turn to page 31.

The stairs leading to the shadowy basement are inviting. Who knows what mysteries could lurk down in this old home's stone foundation?

The steps creak as you slowly descend from one to the next. There was no light switch at the top of the stairs, so you feel your way as best you can. Finally, you step down onto a dirt floor.

You can't see anything, but you find your way to the center of the room. Suddenly, something hits you in the forehead. It's a string of some kind. You smile, feel for the string in the dark, and then pull it. A single lightbulb flickers above you as you look around the cellar.

The room is empty except for an antique furnace built into the far stone wall. Three of the old cellar walls are painted white. But one has been covered with crude wood paneling.

Turn the page.

Suspicious, you carefully inspect each panel. All are cool to the touch except for one. You knock on it and can barely make out the sound of an echo behind it.

You think back to Evan warning you about any damage done to the house.

"What can one wood panel really cost?" you say to yourself.

Then you step back and kick hard at the board. It splinters and breaks under your weight. You instantly feel a draft. In front of you is a narrow stone corridor.

You begin walking down the tunnel. The light is very dim, and it gets harder to see the farther you go. The stones on each side look ancient and are stacked haphazardly. Thick dust kicks up beneath your feet.

A mysterious dark tunnel may lead to hidden treasure.

Turn the page.

When you arrive at the end of the stone corridor, it seems to be a dead end. You reach out and feel the dark wall in front of you.

Two of the old stones in the wall have a small carving engraved on their surface. You can just make out the image of a bird on one of them. You think it might be a swan, but you can't tell for sure. The other is more obvious. It's a carving of a goat.

There is a gap along the outline of each carving. It looks like the animals can be pressed like buttons on some ancient control panel.

You've seen old devices like this before. One of the buttons could open a secret door. The other could activate a booby trap. But which is which?

To press the goat, turn to page 35.
To press the swan, turn to page 37.

The strange trap door in the ceiling of the bedroom has your imagination spinning. You head back upstairs and stand on the bed to examine the wood panel.

There's no cord hanging from it, but when you pry at one end with your fingers, it pulls down easily. You're surprised to see a folding ladder attached to the trapdoor. Exploring the attic will be even easier than you originally thought.

After unfolding the ladder, you slowly begin to climb it. Once at the top, you realize how hot it is in this little attic. There are no windows, and the summer heat seems to be trapped in the small space.

You try to stand up, but the roof is too low. You doubt you'll stay up here for long anyway. The attic is completely empty. There's not even a box of holiday decorations stashed in the corner.

Turn the page.

Just then, the trap door snaps shut behind you. You didn't notice that it was spring-loaded. The ladder folded itself neatly into place, and the door shut behind it.

When you try to open the panel, it won't budge. You put all your weight on the door, but now it's somehow locked tight. Was this an accident, or some kind of strange booby trap?

You wonder if you'll ever find out. Evan won't be back to check on you for weeks. This attic might be the last part of Oak Island you'll ever explore.

THE END

To follow another path, turn to page 11.
To learn more about Oak Island, turn to page 103.

You turn left and head toward the sound of the water. You're not near the beach, so you're curious about what you might find. After a few minutes, you come across a small stream. You follow it downhill until you find a small waterfall. You pause to watch the water pool up below it before continuing on its way. It's a peaceful sight. Whatever unease you were feeling from the shady woods seems to fade away.

But when you look a bit closer at the pool, you see the water is splashing off an oddly-shaped stone. You nearly fall backward in shock. The stone looks exactly like a human skull!

You collect yourself and lean over the creek. You decide to step into the water to get a better look. You see that the stone isn't a real skull. It's just a crudely carved rock. You touch one of its eye sockets and find it strangely smooth. The rock must have been there for hundreds of years.

Turn the page.

You know the stone isn't shaped like this
by accident. So you crouch down in the water
and lift it out of the muck with both hands.
Water begins to pool up in the new, muddy hole
beneath. You can only see the bottom of the hole
for a moment. But that's long enough.

You catch a glimpse of something that looks like wood. You begin to scoop at the hole with your hands, slopping the mud into a pile at the side of the stream. Finally, your hands hit something hard. Something wooden.

You keep digging in the mud until you can get a good grip on the object. Then you yank it backward. The object quickly comes loose from the muck, causing you to fall back into the water with a splash.

On your stomach now rests a heavy wooden trunk. No, it's more than that. It's a treasure chest!

You heave the trunk onto solid ground. But before you can stand up, you hear a man's voice behind you.

"I see that didn't take you very long," says Evan.

Turn the page.

You turn to look at him. He has a gun in his hand. It's pointed right at you.

"I figured you were here for more than just a long vacation. I'll just take that, and then you can be on your way."

He doesn't offer any conversation as he marches you back to the house. He makes you carry the heavy chest the whole way.

You never get to see what's inside. When you check the internet a few weeks later, Evan has taken his house off the rental market. It seems he didn't need the extra income anymore.

THE END
To follow another path, turn to page 11.
To learn more about Oak Island, turn to page 103.

You decide against your better instincts and head down the darker path. You walk for a while, hearing occasional rustling noises behind you.

You wonder if there's any point to staying on a well-worn path. If anything was here, it would have been discovered already. And if someone is following you, you won't lose him out here in the open.

When you hear footsteps, you turn to your right and dart through the thick weeds. You run as fast as you can for several minutes before your foot catches on a jagged root.

You fall to the ground but don't get up right away. Instead, you hold your breath and listen. Everything is quiet. There's no sound aside from the wind blowing through the trees.

Turn the page.

You get to your feet and continue on your way. You pause at times and listen, but you no longer hear footsteps. It was probably all in your head in the first place.

You stop at a thick patch of weeds mingled with thorny bushes. You step as high as you can, but you have to move slowly.

Suddenly, your foot comes down on something hard. It's a small boulder. You push the weeds away to see the famous cross of the Knights Templar engraved on the rock. The symbol is worn and faint with age, but clear just the same.

"This must be some sort of marker," you whisper to yourself.

Then you begin clearing the weeds and thorns away from the large stone. When that's finished, you dig your hands underneath the rock and lift with all your might. It doesn't budge.

An old carving of a cross in stone that looks similar to the Knights Templar cross

Turn the page.

After a few tries, you manage to shift the rock to the side slightly. Finally, it rolls out of place and lands with a crunch in the nearby weeds. Underneath the stone is a large trunk, nearly as big as the boulder itself.

Suddenly, you hear a snap in the weeds behind you. You turn, but don't see anyone. You can't shake the feeling that you're being watched. You're not sure what you should do next.

To dig the trunk out of the dirt, turn to page 41.

To come back later tonight, turn to page 43.

You place your palm on the carving of the goat and press firmly. The goat slides slightly into the wall. But nothing happens.

Then you feel a drip on your forehead. You wipe it off with the back of your hand. Out of curiosity, you smell your hand. It smells like seawater. Then another drip lands on your shoulder.

Suddenly, you feel a light sprinkling on your head, as if it's starting to rain. You look up, and a drop of seawater lands right in your eye. As you blink to clear your vision, the sprinkling becomes a shower.

At that moment, the stone ceiling caves in. Water gushes down on you and knocks you to the ground. You try to get to your feet, but the chamber is flooded before you can move.

Turn the page.

You can't tell which way is up as the water carries you down the hallway. When you slam into a stone slab, you realize what's happened. You've set off an ancient trap, and the tunnel has sealed itself. You gasp for air, but your lungs fill with seawater instead.

The legends of Oak Island say that seven must die before its riches can be uncovered. It looks like you're unlucky number seven.

THE END

To follow another path, turn to page 11.
To learn more about Oak Island, turn to page 103.

Your mind races. You think about the many legends of Oak Island. Some people believe that William Shakespeare is connected to this strange place. They think certain capital letters and misspelled words in his works are a code that refers to a secret stash of treasure in Nova Scotia. That buried treasure could include Shakespeare's own lost manuscripts.

It seems unlikely, but when you see the swan, it's the only theory that seems to make sense. After all, Shakespeare was known as the "Swan of Avon."

You place your hand on the swan and press it. The entire carving moves slightly into the wall. Suddenly, a large section of the stone wall slides open with a rumble.

You step through this new passageway into a small closet-sized chamber. There on the floor is a wooden chest!

Turn the page.

You pick up the chest and walk out of the small chamber. But as you do, you trip over a stone on the floor. You reach out blindly with your free hand and manage to keep yourself from falling.

But then you feel your hand shift into the wall just slightly. You've accidentally pressed the carving of the goat!

One by one, drops of seawater land on your head and shoulders. You know that can't be a good sign. Oak Island has a history of tunnels being flooded by seawater.

With the small chest under your arm, you sprint down the dark hallway toward the cellar. You run through the opening in the wall and back into the basement. Just as you do, a stone slab slides in place to block the tunnel behind you. You hear rushing water on the other side of this new wall.

There's no doubt about it. Pressing the goat carving somehow triggered a trap. The ancient chamber is now filled with seawater. If you hadn't started running, that corridor would have been your watery grave.

You climb the steps back to the main floor of the house. Then you set down the chest on the kitchen counter.

Turn the page.

You feel a rush of excitement as you open the chest's lid. Luckily, not a drop of water damaged the contents inside.

There in the chest is a stack of old parchment paper. On the first page is a neatly written title that reads: *A Storm of Fools*. You've seen this sort of document before. You're looking at a lost play by William Shakespeare!

If there is any other treasure hidden here on Oak Island, it could never compare to the priceless discovery you've just made.

THE END

To follow another path, turn to page 11.
To learn more about Oak Island, turn to page 103.

You decide it's best not to wait, and pull the trunk out of the hole as best you can. You lift the top open and quickly realize why the chest is so heavy. It's full of gold coins—and a golden cup!

You can't believe your eyes. Could the cup be the famous Holy Grail? Did you just find the priceless lost treasure of the Knights Templar?

Turn the page.

This ancient cup, called the Antioch Chalice, was once believed to be the Holy Grail. Some rumors claim that the Knights Templar hid the real Holy Grail somewhere on Oak Island.

Suddenly, a gunshot cracks in the air. You quickly grab two handfuls of coins and shove them into your pockets. Then you grab the cup and take off running. Gunshots follow you for the next few intense moments. You have no idea who is shooting at you.

You make it back to your car unhurt. You jump in, back out of the driveway, and speed down the road as fast as you can.

You don't stop until you're well off Oak Island. Then you pull to the side of the road and collect yourself. You can never go back to the island, but you've made the discovery of a lifetime!

THE END

To follow another path, turn to page 11.
To learn more about Oak Island, turn to page 103.

You quickly cover the trunk with as many thorny vines and weeds as you can find. You take note of the large oak tree towering only a few feet to your right.

Then you stand up and sprint through the woods back to the house. Satisfied that nobody followed you, you unpack your suitcase, fix yourself a meal, and wait for nightfall.

As soon as the sun goes down, you head back out again. You trudge through the woods with only a small flashlight lighting your way. You do your best to retrace your steps. You take the same dark path and then head into the weeds at about the same spot you did earlier.

Finally, you see the large oak tree. You smile from ear to ear. You haven't heard any footsteps this time, but you shine your flashlight all around you just to be safe. There's no one there.

Turn the page.

An old, hollow tree can be a great spot to hide treasure.

You head to the spot in the thick weeds and begin pushing the thorns and brush to either side.

But when you've uncovered the spot, you find only an empty hole. The trunk is gone!

Someone *was* following you earlier. And that someone made off with what could be the answer to the greatest mystery in treasure hunting history. All you can do is head back to the house and start a new hunt tomorrow.

THE END

To follow another path, turn to page 11.
To learn more about Oak Island, turn to page 103.

The Money Pit is thought to be near a small inlet on the island called South Shore Cove.

CHAPTER 3

THE DIG SITE

You wipe your sweaty palms on your pants as you step out of your rental car. You're much more nervous than you thought you'd be.

In front of you is a wide-open area. Little here has been untouched. All the grass and trees have been bulldozed away. Large trucks and enormous drills tower over you. The place feels more like an oil rig than a lonely island with buried treasure.

"There you are!" says a man with a bushy gray beard. He walks toward you and shakes your hand. "Great to finally meet you. I'm James."

"Nice to meet you, too," you say.

"Ready for your first day of work?" James asks, handing you a hard hat.

Turn the page.

"Yes, sir," you say.

"Just to warn you, things on Oak Island rarely go according to plan," James says through a crooked smile. "They say it's all part of the curse."

You return his smile. James seems like a nice guy. But he doesn't know that you're not here to help dig at the fabled Money Pit.

You're a fellow treasure hunter. You've studied this island since you were a kid. You're not sure if the pit holds hidden pirate gold, Marie Antoinette's missing jewels, or the lost plays of William Shakespeare. But you're sure there must be something down there.

When the Money Pit was first discovered, a flat stone was found ninety feet deep in the shaft. An ancient message written in strange characters was said to be carved on the stone.

When decoded, the message roughly said, "Forty feet below two million pounds are buried."

This message seems to be a promise of a large hoard of gold. It has inspired treasure hunters for decades.

A year ago, you bought an old book about Oak Island at an antique auction. You discovered a yellowed piece of paper stuck between its pages.

Turn the page.

Replica of the stone with strange markings that was found in the Money Pit

The paper had an ancient cipher written on it. When you compared it to the flat stone's markings, you believe the message said something else. It translated to say, "Ten feet above, find the tunnel. Go no further."

So, you traveled to Oak Island and found a position on James's crew. But now that you're here, you're not sure you can keep this secret from your new boss. You planned everything out ahead of time, except for the guilt you feel. You're not sure if you should continue on your own or tell James about your discovery.

To tell James the truth, go to page 51.
To keep the cipher a secret, turn to page 53.

The guilt is too much to bear. You decide to tell James about the cipher and your true reasons for being on Oak Island.

After thinking it over for a moment, James finally says, "I didn't expect that. But thank you for telling me. You know, you might have stumbled upon the missing key we've been hunting for."

You and James work out a deal to split any treasure you find. Working together, you stand a much better chance of discovering Oak Island's secrets than working on your own.

The next day, you meet James at the dig site again. He shows you the hole where the oak platforms were discovered long ago by Daniel McGinnis. He and his crew have widened the shaft and have dug it out past the ninety-foot mark.

Turn the page.

At only about six feet wide, the circular pit had been flooded with water. But James and his crew have found a way to drain it to the eighty-foot point. It's only a temporary solution. The water will flood back up to the fifty-foot mark when they switch off their electric pump.

"So, are you coming with us?" James asks as he nods toward the Money Pit. You've always wanted to hunt for this treasure. But now that you're here, it seems riskier than you expected.

To head into the Money Pit, turn to page 55.

To remain at the top as James's crew explores the pit, turn to page 57.

"I'll show you to your new digs and let you get settled in," says James. "Unless you have any questions or anything."

You shake your head no. You'll keep the cipher a secret for now. Then you get back into your rental car and follow James down a narrow road to a small cottage. Once there, he hands you a set of keys. You agree to meet him at the dig site the next morning.

Inside your new temporary home, you unpack your things, have a bite to eat, and then sit nervously on the couch. You can hardly wait until the sun sets. All you can think of is getting back to the Money Pit to start your search.

You wait until it's completely dark outside. Then you get back in your car and drive to the dig site. The workers have long since left. But luckily, their equipment is still here.

Turn the page.

There are two vertical shafts that have been dug at the site. You estimate that each one is about 100 feet deep. James was sure that one of them was the true Money Pit. But he didn't point out which hole that was.

One of the six-foot-wide holes in the ground has a crane positioned over it. Dangling from the crane is a metal platform with an open wire basket around it. You've seen something like this before. The platform is like an elevator used to lower people in and out of a pit.

You shine your flashlight down each pit. The hole with the crane appears flooded far down below. The other appears dry and has a rusty old ladder built into its stone walls.

To try the flooded pit, turn to page 60.
To head down the dry pit, turn to page 63.

You're not about to let James claim all the glory for himself. You're the one who found the cipher, after all. So you gear up with a flashlight and work boots and grab a pickaxe and shovel. Then you step inside the metal basket dangling from a crane above the Money Pit.

You and James can both barely fit on this small metal platform. You give a thumbs up, and the crane operator begins to lower the basket into the Money Pit.

The farther down you go, the darker things get. You take a deep breath. James pats you on the back and smiles. At the eighty-foot point, the platform stops.

"Here we are," says James. "Ten feet above where the flat stone was found. The only question is, where do we dig?"

Turn the page.

You click on your flashlight and scan the tunnel walls around you. You take your shovel and begin tapping it against the stone.

Right away, it sinks in deeper than you thought it would. James does the same on the opposite side of the hole. His shovel also sinks into the wall. You tap at a few more sides of the tunnel, but you don't have the same luck. Your shovel clangs against hard stone.

"Looks like we've narrowed it down to two spots," you say to James.

To dig on your side of the pit, turn to page 66.

To dig on James's side, turn to page 70.

You have no experience working in a cave or mine. Heading into the Money Pit might be best left to the pros.

James, on the other hand, has been at this dig for years. He wastes no time climbing into the metal basket that hangs over the large hole.

Workers often ride in metal cages for safety as they're lowered into mine shafts or other deep holes at dig sites.

Turn the page.

"See you on the other side," he says as the giant crane above him lowers the metal cagelike platform into the pit.

"Good luck," you say. Soon, he's no longer in sight. You look down into the shadowy hole, but all you can see is the faint flicker of his flashlight.

Almost exactly an hour later, you hear something from the pit.

"AUGH!" comes a muffled scream.

"James?" you call down into the shaft. "Are you okay?"

He doesn't answer, but you hear a crash of metal on metal. Then another scream.

"Pull him up!" you yell to the crane operator. It takes a few minutes, but soon, the crane raises the metal basket to the surface. However, James is no longer inside.

You look back down into the pit. The seawater has somehow filled the entire shaft now.

"James!" you yell.

But there's no answer. In fact, you never see James again. Your partner has become the legendary seventh victim of the Oak Island curse.

THE END

To follow another path, turn to page 11.
To learn more about Oak Island, turn to page 103.

The legends maintain that the true Money Pit was flooded after a flat stone was removed at the ninety-foot mark. So the flooded tunnel seems like your best bet. Now you just have to figure out how to get down there.

You climb up into the crane's operating booth. On the floor is a large control box. It looks like a remote control. You're sure it would be safer to rely on a crane operator, but this will have to do.

Your father used to work on construction sites, so you're pretty sure you can operate this system. You turn the crane's key in its ignition and take the control box with you as you step into the basket above the pit. You press the control button, and the platform begins to lower into the dark pit.

Some cranes can be operated with a remote control box.

While you ride down, you use a flashlight to check the water level below you. As you reach the top of the water, you press the control box's off button. But nothing happens!

You press it again, harder this time. But you're still lowering into the water. Out of desperation, you slam the control box into the side of the metal basket.

Turn the page.

The glowing buttons on the remote go dark. But at least the basket stops, and not a moment too soon! The water at the bottom of the pit is now up to your waist.

You try the remote several more times, but it's obviously broken. The chill of the icy cold seawater begins to set in. You call for help, but after yelling for an hour, you don't see the point in it. No one is coming until morning.

You can't stop your body from shivering. You just hope you can stay alive until the sun comes up.

THE END

To follow another path, turn to page 11.
To learn more about Oak Island, turn to page 103.

Your dad was a construction worker. But although you grew up around this sort of equipment, you don't think you can operate the crane remotely and stay safe. So you decide to explore the dry pit.

However, when you set foot on the first rung of the wobbly ladder, you begin to question your choice. With only a flashlight to light your way, you nervously descend dozens of feet into the dark shaft.

Turn the page.

Narrow stairways or ladders are sometimes used to descend into mine shafts.

You have no idea how far down you've gone when you step on a rung that collapses under your weight. The entire bottom section of the rusty ladder gives way! You try to reach out to hold on to something but grasp only air. You fall deep into the pitch-black pit.

You hit the ground with a thud. Luckily, the dirt is soft and helps soften your landing. You're not sure how far you fell or even how deep you are in the pit. You feel around the ground until you discover your flashlight. You switch it on. Thankfully, it still works! At least you have that going for you.

You shine the light around the pit. Stuck in the ground just a foot away from you is the bottom section of the metal ladder. It leans against the wall at a slight angle. But it's completely broken. Half the rungs are missing. You won't be able to get back up the way you came down.

Suddenly, you start to feel a little faint. You steady yourself against the wall. The air seems thicker down here. You feel so tired, you can hardly stand. You lean back against the pit's wall and slide down to the dirt ground. Your eyelids feel heavy. You don't think there's much harm in closing them for a minute or two just to rest.

You remember that Oak Island has many pockets of swamp gas beneath its surface. The gas has claimed two lives previously. As you drift into unconsciousness, you wonder if you are to be the third.

THE END

To follow another path, turn to page 11.
To learn more about Oak Island, turn to page 103.

"Let's start here," you say as you tap your shovel against the wall next to you. James doesn't argue.

For the next hour, you both do your best to pick away at the dirt and stone of the tunnel. The space is so tight that you keep getting in each other's way. Eventually, your shovel sinks into the wall so far that you can barely keep hold of the handle. You've hit a tunnel!

You pull at the surrounding dirt until you've dug a hole about the size of a small window. Without another thought, you squeeze into the space. When you switch on your flashlight again, you're standing in a small stone chamber.

"We've found it!" James says, as he crawls into the chamber behind you. Other than a few odd rock formations, the only thing in the cavern is a small wooden chest.

The chest is half buried in the center of the stone floor. You walk over to it and pry the lid open with your shovel.

Suddenly, water erupts from the open chest. It sprays out like a fountain, quickly covering the ground. It doesn't take long for the small chamber to start filling up.

"Run!" you shout to James.

Turn the page.

You dart toward the hole in the wall. But you slip on the seawater and knock into James. He gets back to his feet first, and pushes through the hole. By now the water is up to your knees—and rising fast!

"Pull us up!" you hear James shout from the other side of the hole. "Hurry!"

The water is so high now, it has started pouring through the hole inside of the main shaft. You try to crawl through the hole, but the water is rushing too quickly.

You stand up and take a few deep breaths as the seawater rises to your chest. Then you dive under the dark water and feel for the hole. You find it and pull yourself through slowly. Your lungs burn as you move. Finally, you manage to squeeze all the way through the hole. You can't see a thing, so you allow yourself to float.

As your head bursts from the surface of the water, you gasp for air. In the shadows above you, you see the metal basket rising toward ground level. James left without you!

But that's not the worst of your problems. The water is causing the pit to become unstable. Rocks and chunks of dirt begin to loosen and fall toward you. Soon, so much earth is falling that you can't see sunlight from the surface any longer. You are buried in the Money Pit—along with its long-held secrets.

THE END

To follow another path, turn to page 11.
To learn more about Oak Island, turn to page 103.

"Let's start on your side," you say to James. You shuffle over next to him and dig your shovel into the soft spot in the wall. The space in the basket is tight, and you both have to take turns with your tools. Together you dig for most of the afternoon.

Finally, your shovel breaks through to something that seems like a tunnel. You dig furiously and make an opening big enough to crawl through.

"Want to do the honors?" you ask James.

Without a word, he pushes past you and into the hole. A moment of silence passes. Then another.

"You okay in there?" you call after James. He doesn't answer.

You gather your nerve. Then you crawl into the hole. You come through the other side into a larger chamber and notice a strange odor. It almost smells like metal. Then a bright light blinds you for a moment. James has switched on his flashlight.

"I thought you'd want the same dramatic reveal I got," he says.

When your eyes adjust, you look around the dimly lit cavern. There is gold everywhere. Gold walls. Gold coins piled on the floor. Gold necklaces encrusted with jewels. This is it. You've found the Money Pit of Oak Island! You wonder if you'll ever stop smiling again.

THE END

To follow another path, turn to page 11.
To learn more about Oak Island, turn to page 103.

A gray, foggy day on the shores of Oak Island

Chapter 4

OFF THE COAST

It would help if it was warmer today. But your wetsuit does a good job of holding your body heat, so you're not too worried.

A chilly day off the coast of Nova Scotia is the least of your problems right now. You're about to embark on the most dangerous treasure hunt of your life.

The crew of the small boat is steering you toward Oak Island. It's a small piece of land you've been studying for years.

Most people think the small island contains only a few homes, a swamp, and a rocky beach or two. But you believe this strange place might hold a link to an ancient treasure of the past.

Turn the page.

Many treasures have been rumored to lurk beneath Oak Island's surface. The stories range from lost religious relics once owned by the Knights Templar, to Marie Antoinette's jewels, to treasure hidden by the infamous pirate Captain Kidd.

The chance of finding treasure is why you've come to the choppy waters of Mahone Bay on this overcast morning. During your research, you learned about two places of interest on the island.

The first is Smith's Cove. Many believe the beach there isn't natural at all. There have been reports of a series of wooden box tunnels that someone built and buried under the sand there.

These wooden tunnels are said to bring ocean water to a flooded treasure chamber located deep under Oak Island. While evidence pointing to the tunnels has been discovered, no one has yet found a major section of this underground system.

Smith's Cove isn't the only fascinating location on Oak Island. You're also interested in a swamp on the other side of the island. Some think that Oak Island used to be not one, but two separate islands. It's possible that a prized treasure was hidden between the two patches of land. Then it was later covered by mud, sand, and dirt. An artificial swamp was the result.

"So where are we headed?" calls out the boat's captain.

You've thought about this hundreds of times. But you're no closer to having an answer. You only have the time and money to follow one of your two leads.

To dive off the coast of Smith's Cove, turn to page 76.

To dive near the swamp, turn to page 79.

Smith's Cove is located on the east side of Oak Island.

"We're heading to Smith's Cove," you call back to the captain.

"Good luck to you then," he says as he steers the boat toward the rocky beach.

When you're close enough, you signal for him to stop. The boat sloshes to a halt. You sit on the side of the boat and secure your oxygen tank and breathing tube. Then you fall backward into the choppy seawater and begin to swim.

With your headlamp to guide you, the trip doesn't take long. Before you know it, you can see the beach in front of you.

Positioned in front of it are rows and rows of large boulders. But there's nothing natural about this rock formation. The boulders look as if they were placed there on purpose.

When you get to the boulders, you guide yourself across the large rock wall. After about ten minutes, one of the rocks shifts beneath your hands.

You roll the rock to the side and look behind it. You see some sort of tunnel between the rocks. It doesn't look man-made, but you can't be sure.

You're about to swim into the small tunnel when you see something out of the corner of your eye. A few yards away is some sort of wooden plank.

Turn the page.

You swim over to it and see that the board is covered with many small stones. You begin to remove the rocks one by one.

Soon enough, you see that the board is a long wooden shaft. It seems to tunnel through the ground for quite a distance.

Could this be one of the rumored box drains that lead to a hidden underground chamber on the island? Possibly.

Or it may be a booby trap left by whoever hid the treasure. You're not sure if you should check out the rock tunnel or the wooden shaft. You must decide soon, or your scuba tank will run out of air.

To swim through the box drain, turn to page 82.

To swim through the tunnel in the rock formation, turn to page 85.

The murky swamp water is separated from Mahone Bay by a thin patch of land. The swamp is in the shape of a *V*. To your eye, it doesn't seem natural at all. It's worth taking a closer look. You tell the boat's captain to steer to the opposite side of Oak Island.

You sit on the edge of the boat and check your scuba gear one last time. Then you flash a thumbs-up at the boat's captain before falling backward into the water.

You begin to kick your feet, using your scuba fins to propel you deeper. Your headlamp shines in front of you, cutting through the darkness.

You reach the base of the island and begin to swim around its rocky wall. After fifteen minutes, you dive a bit deeper. Your tank only holds about forty-five minutes of air. You might have to surface soon if you don't find anything.

Turn the page.

It's hard to see in the dark water, even with your headlamp. But finally, you see a fish disappear through a small crack behind a boulder. You can't help but be a little curious.

When you swim closer, you see the boulder is about the size of a yoga ball. You dig your fingers into the crack and are surprised when the rock easily pulls free. You tug harder, and the boulder rolls away toward the bay's floor.

In front of you is a small tunnel through the rock. Swimming into it, you soon find that the tunnel splits off into two corridors. One is smaller. You would have to be very careful to fit through it with your breathing tank. However, its walls are made of stone.

The other tunnel is larger. You should have no trouble fitting inside. However, it appears to have soft, muddy walls.

To pick the smaller stone tunnel, turn to page 87.

To enter the larger mud tunnel, turn to page 89.

You've heard many stories of Smith's Cove and its legendary box drains. You can't resist seeing one in person, no matter the risk. So you push yourself into the tight space inside the wooden rectangular tunnel.

Swimming through the box drain isn't easy. You're pretty tired by the time you get to the far wall of the wooden tunnel. You're disappointed to see the drain come to such an unexpected end.

In front of you is a mud wall and nothing more. Shining your light around, you notice something odd sticking out of the mud. You look closer and see that they're coconut fibers.

Coconut fibers are mentioned several times in the legends of Oak Island. Coconuts are not native to this part of the world. So finding them here helps confirm the idea that pirates brought them to Oak Island.

If that's true, then there's a good chance that pirates brought their gold here too. It's thought that the coconut fibers help filter out dirt and debris so that only seawater can travel through the box drains.

Knowing this, you begin to dig into the mud with your hands. You move as fast as you can. Your oxygen tank gives you only forty-five minutes of air. By your count, you've already been underwater for thirty minutes.

Your hands quickly rip through the sand and muck. Finally, you dig a hole large enough to pass through into another section of the box drain. You swim faster, worried you'll run out of air.

After a few minutes, you're thrilled to see you've reached the end of the drain. It empties out into a large underwater chamber. You swim into it and shine your headlamp all around.

Turn the page.

You were hoping to find something inside. But what you see is beyond anything you could have imagined.

The underground chamber is flooded with seawater, but that hardly matters. Because the entire cavern is crammed full of gold! Gold coins are piled up so high that you can barely find room to swim between them. Swords with golden handles, piles of precious jewels, and chest after overflowing treasure chest crowd the space.

This is the find of your career. You can't wait to show off your discovery. But you can't decide your next move. One of the chests would be better proof of your discovery. But you're not sure you can carry a heavy chest back with you.

To take only a handful of gold coins, turn to page 94.

To drag the chest back to the surface, turn to page 96.

The box drain could be booby-trapped. Swimming through there by yourself could be dangerous. Instead, you head to the rock formation. You push yourself through the opening in the rocks and begin to swim down the dark tunnel.

It takes only a few minutes to realize you've made a mistake. This tunnel isn't a man-made path at all. And it certainly isn't leading anywhere.

In front of you, the natural tunnel seems to end suddenly. So you do your best to turn around. Unfortunately, the tunnel doesn't allow for much movement. You snag your leg on a sharp rock in the process.

Finally, you manage to turn around. You shine your headlamp at your leg and see a small stream of blood floating into the bay's water.

Turn the page.

You don't think you're hurt too badly, but you don't want to take any chances. You begin to swim toward the opening. But when you shine your light in front of you, a large gray rock seems to be blocking your path. Then the rock moves and opens its tooth-filled jaws.

That's no rock! In front of you is a large, hungry shark. Unfortunately for you, this shark won't be skipping its next meal.

THE END

To follow another path, turn to page 11.
To learn more about Oak Island, turn to page 103.

You've never liked tight spaces, but the mud tunnel just seems too unstable. So, you steady your nerves and swim toward the smaller stone tunnel. To fit inside, you stretch your arms out in front of you. Moving through the tunnel is slow work. Luckily, it's only about twenty feet long. Soon, you're through the worst of it.

At the other end you find the tunnel opens into a large underground pool. You're happy for the chance to move freely in the water. It feels colder here. But you'd rather be cold than stuck.

Turn the page.

Underground caves are sometimes filled with water.

You swim up in the pool until you reach the surface. Looking around with your headlamp, you see you're in a small underground cavern.

You wade out of the pond and remove your mask. The air is musty, but you don't pay it any attention. You're too focused on the name carved into the wall in front of you—Antoinette.

You look around the chamber. Man-made tunnels are carved at opposite ends of the cavern. One cave has the number 16 carved above its entrance. The other has the number 14 above it.

There are rumors of booby traps throughout the island. If you choose the wrong tunnel, it may be the last decision you ever make.

To investigate tunnel 16, turn to page 90.
To choose tunnel 14, turn to page 92.

You swim into the larger corridor. You worry you might get caught in the small stone tunnel. This one seems safer. But as soon as you swim a few feet inside, the water becomes too cloudy to see more than a foot in front of you.

You decide to turn around, but when you do, one of your feet kicks the tunnel's wall. Mud rains down from above until the entire tunnel is blocked off. You try to dig your way out, but it's too hard to see. You're not even sure that you're digging in the right direction.

You can't see the watch on your wrist. But if you could, you'd realize that you have only a few minutes of air left. There are many secrets buried on Oak Island. Now you're one of them.

THE END

To follow another path, turn to page 11.
To learn more about Oak Island, turn to page 103.

You remove your swim fins, oxygen tank, and a few other bulky items. Then you head toward tunnel 16. Marie Antoinette was married to King Louis XVI. So that tunnel makes the most sense to you.

When the French Revolution began, both Marie and her husband were chased from their palace. Rumors say she trusted her valuable jewels to a maid who brought them to North America. If you do find jewels in this tunnel, you will have discovered a major historical find.

You shine your headlamp ahead of you as you walk steadily down the dark cave. Suddenly, the cavern ends. There, against the wall in front of you, is a small wooden chest. The wood looks rotted with age.

You open the chest carefully. But there are no jewels inside. Instead, there is just a single piece of paper.

It reads:

We regret to inform you that the treasure has already been found. Do not look up.

By the time you look above you, you notice a worn rope attached to the lid of the wooden chest. You realize that you were right about the booby traps, even if you were wrong about the tunnel number. It comes as little comfort as the ceiling caves in on you.

THE END

To follow another path, turn to page 11.
To learn more about Oak Island, turn to page 103.

You don't know much about the former queen of France named Marie Antoinette. But you do know that she was married at age fourteen. So you choose the tunnel marked 14 and hope for the best.

Marie Antoinette

Marie Antoinette and her husband, King Louis XVI, fled from their palace when the people rose against them during the French Revolution. You've read that the queen may have trusted a loyal maid with her jewels. That maid is rumored to have traveled all the way to North America to hide the precious gems. The carved "Antoinette" on the wall seems to confirm her journey.

You're excited by what you might find in the tunnel. But that excitement suddenly turns to panic when your light shines on a skeleton slumped against the far wall of the cave.

After you collect yourself, you move in for a closer look. The skeleton is clutching a small cloth pouch. A wooden chest rests next to the skeleton on the cave floor. Either could hold a clue to the treasure of Marie Antoinette.

To inspect the cloth pouch, turn to page 98.
To open the chest, turn to page 100.

You're too tired as it is. You could never manage to lug a treasure chest back to the surface with you. So you grab some gold coins with each hand and swim back toward the box drain.

You check your oxygen level as you swim back through the wooden drain. Everything looks good, but you only have a few minutes of air left. So it's more than a little scary when a plank from the box drain's ceiling collapses down in the tunnel ahead of you.

As quickly as you can, you try to push the board back into position. But you can't move it with your hands full of the gold coins.

You have no choice. You must drop the coins to move the wooden plank. Using all your strength, you push the plank up just high enough to swim under it. You kick your feet as hard as you can. You're nearly out of air!

As you swim, you glance back over your shoulder. With the help of your headlamp, you can see the box drain tunnel caving in completely behind you.

You burst from the drain's opening just as the whole structure gives way. Where the box drain once sat between the rocks, there now sits a pile of rubble.

Any hope of swimming back for the gold is buried under tons of stone and wood. You didn't recover a single coin. There is treasure buried under Oak Island. But you won't be the one to bring it home.

THE END

To follow another path, turn to page 11.
To learn more about Oak Island, turn to page 103.

You didn't come this far to have your discovery questioned. You need real proof that you've uncovered the treasure of Oak Island.

You grab one of the treasure chests by its handle and begin dragging it back down the box drain the way you came. To your credit, you make it halfway down the drain before you have to give up. The treasure chest is just too heavy.

You leave the chest where it is and decide to swim back to the surface for a break. You need to go back to the boat and change oxygen tanks. The treasure will still be there when you get back.

But as you swim the rest of the way down the wooden tunnel, you start to feel lightheaded. You're not sure if you've run out of oxygen or have simply tired yourself out.

But when you pause to catch your breath, you can't seem to keep your eyes open.

I just need . . . a quick . . . break, you think.

But it feels too good to close your eyes and rest.

So much so that you never open your eyes again.

THE END

To follow another path, turn to page 11.
To learn more about Oak Island, turn to page 103.

The pouch couldn't possibly hold all of Marie Antoinette's jewels. But you decide to see what's inside it anyway.

As gently as you can, you reach into the skeleton's hand. You pinch the small cloth pouch between your index finger and thumb. Then you slowly pull it from the grip of the ancient bones.

Suddenly, the cave begins to shake. It feels as if the ceiling will cave in on you. You think about running back to the underground pool when you notice that the floor itself is sinking.

As if triggered by some ancient pulley system, the floor drops two feet down into the cave. A small opening can now be seen behind the skeleton.

You shine your headlamp through this square hole and see a large chamber on the other side. Falling to your stomach, you slide through.

You can hardly believe what you see next. In front of you are three old wooden chests. Each one overflows with jewels and gold.

You've done the impossible. You found Marie Antoinette's jewels, and another fortune in gold besides! If Oak Island holds any other secrets, you have no desire to find them. This treasure is the discovery of a lifetime.

THE END

To follow another path, turn to page 11.
To learn more about Oak Island, turn to page 103.

There's no better place to find treasure than inside a treasure chest. So your choice seems like an easy one.

You kneel down beside the skeleton and reach toward the chest. The wood is covered in a slimy green mold. You put one hand on either side of the lid and lift it. An ancient hinge screeches in protest. But the lid opens just the same.

"What?" you say out loud in disbelief. The chest is empty!

You reach into the chest and feel its fabric lining. Then your heart starts racing again. It's a false bottom!

You pull at its corners, and the bottom of the chest pops right out. That's when you hear a click. Suddenly, the chest explodes, sending you flying across the tunnel and into the hard stone wall. The chest was booby-trapped!

You look up and realize that the ringing in your head is the least of your problems. The entire ceiling is caving in above you. You try to get to your feet, but you don't have time. Perhaps years from now, someone will find not one skeleton in this cave, but two.

THE END

To follow another path, turn to page 11.
To learn more about Oak Island, turn to page 103.

Young Franklin D. Roosevelt (third from right) searched for the Oak Island treasure in the early 1900s.

CHAPTER 5

THE LURE OF THE ISLAND

The possibility of hidden treasure on Oak Island has long captivated people around the world. President Franklin D. Roosevelt was one such treasure hunter. Long before becoming president, a younger Roosevelt tried to discover the island's hidden secrets. But like most who have searched the island, Roosevelt came up empty.

Over the years, six people have died while searching for Oak Island's rumored riches. Two were killed due to machinery malfunctions. Two were overcome by deadly natural gas found under the island's soil. Two others drowned while searching flooded dig sites. It's often said that anything that can go wrong on Oak Island most surely will.

Marty (left) and Rick (right) Lagina have been searching for Oak Island's mysterious lost treasure since 2006.

Perhaps the most famous Oak Island treasure hunters are featured on the popular TV program *The Curse of Oak Island.* Brothers Rick and Marty Lagina share a childhood obsession with Oak Island's mysteries. They've spent millions of dollars trying to excavate various locations on the island.

But after several years, the Laginas have found only a few hints of gold, some ancient coins and buttons, and a few antique trinkets. They have yet to locate one of the legendary artifacts rumored to be stashed away on the island.

If treasure was ever on Oak Island, is it still there today? Nobody is sure. Some historians think that former Oak Island landowner Samuel Ball may have found the treasure on his property and taken it long ago.

Oak Island continues to lure people to its shores every day. It attracts those that dream of discovering a fortune, as well as those who wish to unlock a hidden chapter of history.

Oak Island may not hold pirate gold, lost manuscripts, fabled jewels, or the Holy Grail. But it does have one thing that's impossible for many people to resist—a real mystery that has yet to be solved.

MYSTERIES OF OAK ISLAND

There are few areas of Oak Island that have been left untouched over the years. This map shows some of the most famous points of interest on Oak Island that have kept treasure hunters guessing for decades.

THE CAUSEWAY

This man-made road allows people easy passage to and from the island.

THE STONE CROSS
This giant boulder formation might link the island to the Knights Templar, a wealthy and mysterious religious order that was active in the Middle Ages.

THE SWAMP
Some believe Oak Island's swamp is man-made and hides a buried treasure chamber.

SMITH'S COVE
Rumors say that pirate treasure may lurk under the surface of this mysterious beach.

THE MONEY PIT
More than one treasure hunter has tried to unlock the secrets of this ninety-foot pit. None have succeeded.

BOREHOLE 10X
This tunnel was dug after the Money Pit was flooded. It may hold secrets of its own.

OTHER PATHS TO EXPLORE

>>> Some people believe that Oak Island isn't the true home
to the pirate gold of Captain Kidd. There are more than
300 small islands in Mahone Bay. Any one of them could
hide ancient treasures. If you chose to search these islands,
how would you decide where to look? Would you search
old books for clues? Would you talk to locals to see what
legends they've heard?

>>> Several books have been written that connect Oak Island
to the religious order called the Knights Templar. Some
believe the island was only one place the Templar hid
their prized relics. Imagine finding a map that proved
the Templars intended to bury their gold on the island.
How would you search for the treasure? If you found lost
relics, would you donate them to a museum, or would you
try to sell them for profit?

>>> A few treasure hunters and historians believe the Rosslyn
Chapel in Scotland offers clues that link Oak Island to
lost treasures. Corn was not a native crop in Scotland, yet
it seems to be featured on decorations inside the church.
Some think this proves that the Knights Templar visited
Canada. What other clues might link the chapel to the
so-called "New World" of North America? What evidence
might you uncover that could disprove the connection?

BIBLIOGRAPHY

Burns, Kevin, executive producer. *The Curse of Oak Island*. Prometheus Entertainment, History Channel, 2014–2022.

Crooker, William S. *Oak Island Gold: Startling New Discoveries in the World's Most Famous Treasure Hunt*. Halifax, Nova Scotia: Nimbus Publishing Limited, 1993.

Sora, Steven. *The Lost Treasure of the Knights Templar: Solving the Oak Island Mystery*. Rochester, VT: Destiny Books, 1999.

GLOSSARY

causeway (KAWZ-way)—a raised road or paved path used to cross low or wet ground

cipher (SY-fuhr)—a code that uses letters or symbols to represent letters of the alphabet

corridor (KOHR-uh-dohr)—a long, narrow passage or hallway inside a building or structure

excavation (ek-skuh-VAY-shuhn)—the process of digging material out of the ground to look for certain objects, such as at an archaeological site

frequent (FREE-kwuhnt)—to visit a location often

haphazardly (hap-HAH-zuhrd-lee)—random and lacking organization

infamous (IN-fuh-muhs)—known for a negative act or a bad reputation

instinct (IN-stingkt)—behavior or actions that are natural rather than learned

overcast (OH-vuhr-kast)—gray and cloudy

unconsciousness (un-KON-shuhss-ness)—not awake or alert; being unaware of what is happening around you

READ MORE

Hamilton-Barry, Joann. *Oak Island and the Search for Buried Treasure*. Halifax, Nova Scotia: Nimbus Publishing, 2015.

Manning, Matthew K. *Can You Find the Knights Templar Treasure? An Interactive Treasure Adventure*. North Mankato, MN: Capstone Press, 2024.

Stefoff, Rebecca. *Captain Kidd*. New York: Cavendish Square Publishing, 2015.

INTERNET SITES

All The Treasure Ever Found On The Curse of Oak Island
looper.com/748269/all-the-treasure-ever-found-on-the-curse-of-oak-island/

Oak Island Mystery
oakislandmystery.com/the-mystery/introduction-to-oak-island

Oak Island Treasure
oakislandtreasure.co.uk/

ABOUT THE AUTHOR

Author photo courtesy of
Dorothy Manning Photography.

Matthew K. Manning is the author of more than 100 books and dozens of comic books. Some of his favorite projects include the popular comic book crossover *Batman/Teenage Mutant Ninja Turtles Adventures* and the 12-issue series *Marvel Action: Avengers* for IDW, *Exploring Gotham City* for Insight Editions, and the six-volume chapter book series *Xander and the Rainbow-Barfing Unicorns* for Capstone. Manning lives in Asheville, North Carolina, with his wife, Dorothy, and their two daughters, Lillian and Gwendolyn. Visit him online at www.matthewkmanning.com.